PROPHETIC SUPERNATURAL STREAMS

FROM FATHER'S HEART TO YOURS

DR. APRIL GRISETA

ISBN 978-1-0980-8196-6 (paperback)
ISBN 978-1-0980-8197-3 (digital)

Christian Faith Publishing, Inc.
832 Park Avenue
Meadville, PA 16335
www.christianfaithpublishing.com

Printed in the United States of America

Contents

A Personal Message from the Author

This is a basic introduction to prophetic ministry. What is taught is substantiated by the Word of God (a surer word of prophecy). Danger comes in when "revelations" are not backed up by the Word of God. There is safety in the confines of God's Word. It is not of any private interpretation. While God does speak through dreams and visions, those dreams and visions must align with the overall precepts of God's whole counsel. Manifestations of the Holy Spirit will also line up with the Word of God. The Word of God is the plumb line by which we can judge the authenticity of the spoken prophetic word. If it contradicts the Word, it can be discounted as it most likely is coming from the soul or demonic realm. Speaking the truth in love is another determining factor if something is of God or not. God is love.

It is my hope that the readers will mature in the message of righteousness and not be tossed to and fro by every wind and wave that sweeps through the church.

Hebrews 5:13–14 says, "For everyone who lives on milk is still an infant, inexperienced in the message of righteousness. But solid food is for the mature who by constant use have trained their sensibilities to distinguish good from evil."

May you grow in the grace and knowledge of our Lord Jesus Christ, and may the Lord increase you more and more as you diligently study to show yourselves approved unto God.

Introduction

There have been many questions regarding prophets and prophetic ministry. Questions such as the following are often asked: Is it from God or the devil? Is it for today, or was it only for the early church? Are New Testament prophets different from Old Testament prophets? Can New Testament prophets bring words that are not comforting? Throughout this book, we will thoroughly explain the origin of the prophetic and view the Scriptures to validate prophetic gifting today.

It is my aim to uncloud the mystery behind this supernatural gifting of the Holy Spirit. Prophecy is not a gift of the Spirit we ever want to quench. It is vital for the strengthening of the body of believers. Many churches have refused to allow this gift to operate and in doing so have grieved the Holy Spirit. We never want to dampen or snuff out the Holy Spirit's fire.

Without the gifts of the Holy Spirit (prophecy being one of the nine found in 1 Corinthians 12:7–11), the churches are left with little power. This has disturbed me greatly and has spurred the writing of this book. It is the Holy Spirit who distributes the gifts as He wills for the profit withal, and He must be allowed to do so. The church belongs to God, and only He knows exactly what we need to mature in Him.

We need the word of wisdom through the Spirit; we need the word of knowledge through the same Spirit. We also need faith, gifts of healing, working of miracles, *prophecy*, discerning of spirits, diverse tongues, and interpretation of tongues (see 1 Corinthians 12:7–11). The church is to be alive, moving in revelation and miraculous power.

It is interesting that discerning of spirits is right next to prophecy. Many who move in the prophetic also operate in the gift of discernment. This means they can see that which is unseen and can distinguish what spirit is operating. They can tell if it is of the flesh, of the demonic, or of the Spirit.

I have personally found churches that do not allow the Holy Spirit to flow to be very dry. Naturally so, as the Holy Spirit breathes life and brings creative dynamic activity into the congregation.

Have you ever wondered why a leader would not want the moving of the Spirit? I think this is a very fair question and something to look at. Does the leader want control? Is there something he is trying to hide, or does the supernatural make him feel inadequate or awkward? Or is it simply because of some bad experiences that occurred when flesh arose? I do not believe shutting out the Holy Spirit's gifts is the answer and will cause more harm than good. While there has been some kooky stuff, this does not disqualify the genuine.

This book has been created to acquaint believers with the purpose, passion, and protocols of prophetic ministry. We want to look at Father's will for His church, His heart to encourage, and His design for order. Upon completion of the reading of this book, you will be able to distinguish the true heart and function of the office of the prophet and prophetic ministry. You will also have a greater understanding of the preparation of the prophet and the satanic attacks that come against them. Finally, you will learn about spiritual abuse and how trauma can impact the prophetic minister.

My Start in Prophetic Ministry

There are a lot of misperceptions regarding prophetic ministry, and I believe with the help of the Holy Spirit, greater clarity and revelation will come. The Holy Spirit guides into all truth and imparts wisdom and revelation. He brings understanding.

Before I received Jesus as my Lord and Savior, I was given a Bible. It was just sitting by the nightstand, so I decided to read the first four gospels of the New Testament. After reading it, I threw the book down and said to myself, *They all say the same thing.* A week later, I was born again and read those four gospels again. I could not believe how they were so different. The Holy Spirit opened the Scriptures to me. I was so amazed. I was so filled with love and became so hungry to learn more of Jesus. I wanted everything that God wanted me to have.

I was baptized in the Holy Ghost and was water baptized within a month of salvation. The night I received the baptism of the Holy Spirit, I saw heaven open and pour out silver rain into me, and then my beautiful prayer language came flowing out in a beautiful song. No one laid hands on me to receive the gift of the Holy Spirit. It happened while I was worshipping. This demonstrates that Jesus is the baptizer and not man.

Everything looked so different after I received Jesus. The streets of Brooklyn looked clean, and the trees appeared as if they were clapping for me as I skipped down the street. The sky looked bluer than I have ever seen it. Everything looked brand new. I felt so clean and knew in my heart that God gave me a fresh start. I finally was able to feel joy and had lightness of heart. People even noticed a shine on my face.

People's faces in the church also shined, and they prayed in different languages. They danced with all their might and raised their hands in the assembly. This was quite a different experience for me. I grew up in a Catholic home and went to religious instructions every week. Church was kind of boring back then.

My grandfather who was an alcoholic would take me to church on Sunday. He wore a winter coat in the summer, and a bottle of wine could always be found in his pocket. He usually wore his Siamese cat around his neck but not to church. I loved my grandfather deeply and am grateful that he was one of the first ones to plant a seed about the knowledge of God.

Before coming to the Lord, I drank very heavily. I would often go to a deli to buy beer. One day, I looked down on the counter and saw a flyer. On this flyer was a picture of Jesus, and the caption was "Behold the Man." This was an Easter play given by a church. It so intrigued me that I asked the deli owner to take me to the play. It was my first encounter with the Living God. I remember trembling while watching Jesus hang on a bloody cross. The reality of God was so awakening. His presence filled the room.

I could hardly wait for the next service. It was during a midweek service where I ran down the aisle and received Jesus as my Lord and Savior. My life was never again the same. I found the love I so desperately searched for all my life. Alcohol went, cigarettes went, and panic attacks left after my new birth. Most of my friends left too because they lost their drinking buddy. I, however, never felt the loss because what I received was so much greater. Apostle Paul (inspired by the Holy Spirit) wrote, "Yes, everything else is worthless when compared with the infinite value of knowing Christ Jesus my Lord. For his sake I have discarded everything else, counting it all as garbage, so that I could gain Christ" (Philippians 3:18 NLT).

I found myself knowing things that really could not be known in the natural. I would know what the preacher's sermon would be. I would know if a person was genuine or not. I would sense different types of atmospheres and clearly see the demonic before it would manifest. God would also show me broken hearts and distinguish whether it was grieving a loss, relational pain, or family trouble.

God does reveal secrets to His servants and prophets when God deems them trustworthy. He simply will not share secrets if you use the information to harm others. He even tells us not to cast our pearls to swine or give that which is holy to the dogs (Matthew 7:6). This says there are pearls and who not to give them to.

God promised Jeremiah that if he would call to him, not only would He answer him but also "He would reveal to him great and mighty things that could not otherwise be known. The word *mighty* (Hebrew batsar) is better rendered isolated or inaccessible. The suggestion is that God would give Jeremiah revelation insight—revealing things that otherwise would be inaccessible or isolate."[1]

God wants to use you to bless others. He will give you words of encouragement to build up the body. He is a gift giver and gives generously.

If you eagerly desire to move more in the gifts, pray:

> *Father, I desire to be a blessing to others. I would like to operate in the gifts of the Holy Spirit. I choose to live a life holy unto You and bring glory unto You. In Jesus's name, amen.*

---

[1] Jack Hayford, New *Spirit-Filled Life Bible* (Nashville, TN: Thomas Nelson Inc., 2002), 1007.

Beginning to Move in the Spirit

The members of the church that I was attending moved in the gifts of the Spirit. I wanted that. The first thing I remember before really moving in the prophetic ministry was such a desire for it. If you want to move in the prophetic, the Bible says to eagerly desire to prophesy.

> Pursue love, and desire spiritual *gifts,* but especially that you may prophesy. For he who speaks in a tongue does not speak to men but to God, for no one understands *him;* however, in the spirit he speaks mysteries. But he who prophesies speaks edification and exhortation and comfort to men. He who speaks in a tongue edifies himself, but he who prophesies edifies the church. (1 Corinthians 14:1–4 NKJV)

However, before the Word states to eagerly desire spiritual gifts, it states to pursue love. The gifts of the Spirit are birthed out of God's heart of love and care for His creation. All ministry should launch from love. For without love, we do not have anything and will be as clanging cymbals.

> If I speak in the tongues of men or of angels, but do not have love, I am only a resounding gong or a clanging cymbal. If I have the gift of prophecy and can fathom all mysteries and all knowledge,

and if I have a faith that can move mountains, but do not have love, I am nothing. If I give all I possess to the poor and give over my body to hardship that I may boast, but do not have love, I gain nothing. (1 Corinthians 13:1–3 NIV)

If one wants to prophesy, one should have a deep love for the brethren. If they are going to speak on Father's behalf, they must represent His heart. God is love.

What Is Prophecy?

Prophecy is divinely inspired (God-breathed) spoken words that edify, encourage, and comfort. It can declare what will happen in the future but does not necessarily have to. Prophecy is to communicate God's words and God's heart as He reveals them to us. It is a gift of the Holy Spirit who comforts us, guides us into all truth, and shows us things to come through prophetic revelation.

But the Comforter, which is the Holy Ghost, whom the Father will send in my name, he shall teach you all things, and bring all things to your remembrance, whatsoever I have said unto you. (John 14:26 KJV)

Howbeit when he, the Spirit of truth, is come, he will guide you into all truth: for he shall not speak of himself; but whatsoever he shall hear, that shall he speak: and he will shew you things to come. (John 16:13 KJV)

Prophecy can also reveal the secrets of one's thoughts and intents—so much so that where the person being prophesied to will truly declare that God is among them. (Why? Because only God could have known those things about them.)

> And thus the secrets of his heart are revealed;
> and so, falling down on his face, he will worship
> God and report that God is truly among you.
> (1 Corinthians 14:25 NKJV)

I have been in services where the pastor would look at someone new in the congregation and prophesy things that were going on in their life down to minute details. These were only known to God and the one being prophesied to. They walked away knowing God was with us.

Prophetic words come from the Holy Spirit as opposed to psychics who get their information from the demonic realm (from the prince of the power of the air and familiar spirits). Demon spirits have been studying you and your family for some time. They have collected "generation information." They are not all-knowing like God nor are they omnipresent.

I want to point out that Christians should be incredibly careful to what they open themselves up to. Have you ever thought what happens when you are emptying your mind during transcendental meditation? Could something else be coming in? How about when you watch filth on TV? Christians must protect their eye and ear gates. They are responsible as to what they allow in the temple.

> Know ye not that your body is the temple of the
> Holy Ghost. (1 Corinthians 6:19 KJV)

Christians are to be holy, for God is holy. They are separated unto God and are no longer to conform to the ways of this world. God did not look favorably on those who sought out counsel from mediums or other sources (see Isaiah 47:13).

Unbelievers, however, are seeking the supernatural. They are looking for existential answers: Why am I here? What is my purpose? etc. Many are just looking in the wrong places for the answers. Believers need to tell unbelievers that Jesus is the way, the truth, and the life, and no one can come unto the Father but by Him (John 14:6). Jesus is the answer.

As a kid, I was always interested in the supernatural. I played around with Ouija boards and tarot cards. There is a seducing spirit working behind these things, and it appeals to human intrigue. It has to do with arousing the curiosity.

There is nothing new under the sun. The serpent used the same tactics in the garden of Eden as he aroused Eve's interest to be like God.

The Difference Between Prophet and Prophecy?

All may prophesy, but not all are appointed to the office of the prophet. We can all operate in the gift of prophecy as the Spirit wills and distributes the gifts. We also can operate in the other gifts of the Holy Spirit as found in 1 Corinthians 12:8–11 NKJV.

> For to one is given the word of wisdom through the Spirit, to another the word of knowledge through the same Spirit, to another faith by the same Spirit, to another gifts of healings by the same Spirit, to another the working of miracles, to another prophecy, to another discerning of spirits, to another different kinds of tongues, to another the interpretation of tongues. But one and the same Spirit works all these things, distributing to each one individually as He wills.

We are not all, however, called prophets. If someone is called a prophet, then you are looking at a ministry office. It is part of the fivefold ministry gifts as found in Ephesians 4:11 KJV.

> And He gave some apostles, and some, prophets and some evangelists and some pastors and teachers.

The office of the prophet is a governmental gift to the body and helps bring instruction, guidance, and warning to the church. They often work closely with the apostle or leader of the house. The five ministry offices (apostles, prophets, evangelists, pastors, and teachers) are also known as "ascension gifts" that Christ gave for the nurturing and the equipping of the church.

> This is why it says, when he ascended on high, he took many captives and gave gifts to his people. (Ephesians 4:8 NIV)

Dr. Stuart Pattico in his blog "The Difference Between the Gift of Prophecy and the Office of the Prophet" notes the following:

> As the name "prophet" suggests, prophesying will be the dominant feature of a prophet's ministry. To prophesy simply means to speak forth a revelation we have personally received from God (the Greek word literally means to "speak forth"). Whereas all believers can prophesy, prophecy will not necessarily be the dominant feature of that believer's ministry (e.g. a teacher may prophesy from time to time, but his or her ministry will be dominated by teaching). But if they are a prophet, his or her ministry will be dominated by the prophetic! Prophets are continuously speaking forth revelations that they have received from God.[2]

---

[2] Stuart Pattico, "The Difference Between the Gift of Prophecy and the Office of the Prophet," www.stuartpattico.com, April 2017.

Soul Wounds and Prophecy

If you are to prophesy, you should be healed in your heart. If you are wounded, you just may speak out of your own pain and not God's heart. Soul wounds have a way of clouding vision. This unfortunately can taint your ability to accurately discern the voice of God. There once was a prophetess I knew who was so hurt by a Jezebel spirit; she began to see all women as Jezebels. She was not perceiving accurately, and her prophecies were off.

Severely depressed prophetic ministers may carry negativity which will manifest in his/her prophetic stream. For out of the abundance of the heart, the mouth will speak. In the counseling field, they have developed a concept called *transference*. Transference is simply a transfer of one person's emotions to another, but I have found transference impacts atmospheres as well.

I have gone to meetings where there was an oppression in the air. Sometimes it was "carried in" by those housing it, and other times, it was a result of witchcraft praying. Either way, it could never stay in a room filled with praying spirit-filled believers. Why? Because greater is He within us than he that is in the world (1 John 4:4). Also, believers who are submitted to God will resist the devil, and he must flee (James 4:7).

Bitterness and unforgiveness are also major hinderances and pollutants. Prophetic ministers who are bitter will have a murky spring. Can both fresh water and salt water flow from the same spring? My brothers and sisters, can a fig tree bear olives or a grapevine bear figs? Neither can a salt spring produce fresh water (James 3:11–12 NIV). Prophetic streams that come out of wounded hearts can be extremely dangerous as it will defile many.

> Looking carefully lest anyone fall short of the grace of God; lest any root of bitterness springing up cause trouble, and by this many become defiled. (Hebrews 12:15 NKJV)

I have seen young prophetic ministers fall into charismatic witchcraft (conjuring a word) and tell people what they want to hear, simply to be accepted. These young ministers need training on who they are in God and their position in the family of God. They have already been made accepted in the Beloved (Ephesians 1:6 NKJV) and have been made joint heirs with Christ (Romans 8:17 NKJV). They do not have to do anything to be accepted. This was done for them at the cross of Calvary.

Some have felt "pressured" to deliver a word and have prophetically misfired. Prophesy on demand can place pressure on young ministers to perform. People should just simply come up for prayer, and if the Lord should use the minister to prophesy, praise God. I personally cannot stand when people come on the lines with their recorders—talk about pressure to perform—yikes. Why not trust the Holy Spirit to quicken back to you what was spoken by His spirit?

In any event, if you move in the prophetic, you cannot be a people pleaser. You must speak only what God gives you. Do not add or take away from the word He gave you to deliver. Young ministers sometimes feel the need to embellish if it is a short word. Please remember we are all imperfect people. By the mouth of two or three witnesses, let every word be established (2 Corinthians 13:1). There is safety in this guideline.

There was once a prophetess that would visit, and every time there was a selah in worship, she would say God loves you. While this is true, it was not what God was saying at that moment. The other prophets judged and agreed.

Some people just want to bring attention to themselves. Prophetic ministers point people Godward. They look to exalt Jesus and bring glory to Him, not themselves. We must be able to distinguish the motive of the heart.

I would ask every believer to pray for the gift of discerning of spirits. This is one way of knowing if something is of the devil, the flesh, or of God. We must also have our senses exercised through the Word of God to discern between good and evil.

> But solid food is for the mature, who by constant
> use have trained themselves to distinguish good
> from evil. (Hebrews 5:14 KJV)

We know that every good and perfect gift comes from above. The prophetic is a good gift not to be dismissed because there has been some kookiness. Therefore, the word must be judged by other prophets.

> Every good gift and every perfect gift is from
> above, and cometh down from the Father of
> lights, with whom is no variableness, neither
> shadow of turning. (James 1:17 KJV)

Two or three prophets should speak, and the others should weigh carefully what is said (1 Corinthians 14:29 NIV).

Determining What Is My Stuff and What Is Your Stuff

I believe it is especially important that the prophetic vessel knows themselves well and can properly prophesy. They will have to know whether they are picking up on other people's stuff or it is their own stuff interfering with perception.

I have experienced transference and countertransference in the prophetic prayer lines. What that means is this: I have felt other people's emotions (transference), but there have been times where their emotions triggered my own resolved pain. My understanding of the concept of countertransference is wounds banging into wounds. The person's pain triggers the unhealed areas of the prophet. It is said, "If the emotion leaves rather quickly, it was transference but if it stays, it is countertransference."

I share this here because we, as a body, can be affected by other members of the body. I believe it is so important that prophetic ministers invite God daily to search their hearts. The psalmist welcomed the search of the heart.

> Investigate my life, O God, find out everything about me; Cross-examine and test me, get a clear picture of what I'm about; See for yourself whether I've done anything wrong—then guide me on the road to eternal life. (Psalm 139:23–24 MSG).

The Holy Spirit will reveal that which is hidden. He will disclose your own wounds. God wants you whole.

If you know in your heart that you have unresolved wounds, please pray,

> *Father, I welcome you to search my heart and reveal all my wounds that need tending to. Help me to be courageous through the exploration and make the changes as directed by your Spirit. In Jesus's name, amen.*

Benefits and Impact of the Prophetic Ministry

There are many benefits of prophesying. The first benefit I would like to mention is prospering. Prophetic ministers often come alongside of a work to help bring it to completion or fulfillment. It can be a shoring up type of ministry. Often, when a work is at a standstill, God will send prophetic ministers to herald the messages of God. They will bring clarity of vision. "They will begin to give practical and visible effect to the noble prophecies dictated by the Spirit."[3]

> And the elders of the Jews builded, and they prospered through the prophesying of Haggai the prophet and Zechariah the son of Iddo. And they builded, and finished it, according to the commandment of the God of Israel, and according to the commandment of Cyrus, and Darius, and Artaxerxes king of Persia. (Ezra 6:14 KJV)

Prophets have come to our church and proclaimed the word of the Lord. Immediately after, people wanted to volunteer and reported having a new fire for service. Others reported repenting.

The second benefit I would like to mention is prophesying leads to activation. Prophets come with *activating power*. The true prophetic brings activation. We know that Ezekiel spoke as com-

---

[3] Joseph Parker, *The People's Bible: Discourses on Holy Scripture*, "Prophets and Builders," Ezra v, vi. p.172.

manded by the Lord, and the dry bones came alive. That which was dry and desiccated with no hope came alive (see Ezekiel 37:1–14). I have heard of prophets coming to a region and it being transformed because he or she declared the word of God according to His command. We know that Elijah being a natural man prayed, and it rained, and crops were produced (James 5:17–18).

Prophetic ministers that do not spend time in the secret place with God will not receive secrets or things they know not. We must call unto Him, and He will show things that could not otherwise be accessed. If they do not hear from God, they will most likely speak about themselves or tell a bunch of stories to captivate their audience. They even may start to *name-drop* hoping their affiliations will impress you. This, of course, is foolishness. We have already been made famous in our Father's sight.

A prophetic minister who has bathed himself in prayer and comes speaking under the unction of the Holy Spirit will have evidence. He or she will come with the demonstration of the Spirit's power. They will be walking with kingdom authority and know who they are in their God. They know they are a royal priesthood. They know they are kings and priests unto God. Finally, they know the power of their words.

The kingdom of God is not only powerful but voice activated. We know that the earth was without form and void, and then God spoke. He spoke light and life into existence. The spoken Word of God can create and establish. We read how the Spirit of God (the Ruach Ha Kodesh) hovered over the earth with creative, dynamic activity (see Genesis 1:2 NKJV). He is the executive arm of the Trinity. He was hovering. He was not stationary. The Holy Spirit looks to bring chaos into cosmos or *order*.[4] God is a God of order and will use His ministers to speak and bring things into alignment.

As I was just writing, I got a mental snapshot of Christ walking in the midst of the seven golden lampstands... He was "walking" through and bringing instruction to the churches. Prophetic snap-

---

[4] Jack Hayford. *New Spirit Filled Life Bible* (Nashville, TN: Thomas Nelson Inc., 2002) 4.

shots are sometimes given to prophetic vessels or seers. While this can be found in Revelation 2:1, the Lord highlighted it to me now to demonstrate the role of the prophet.

Jesus now sends prophets to help bring proper alignment and restoration to His church. In the Old Testament, we find Ezekiel speaking to dry bones to come alive and properly align. The situation (the dry bones) is changed by the spoken word as commanded by the Lord.

Prophets come with restoring power for the purpose of equipping and maturing the church. The fragmented bones in the story of Ezekiel were made whole, and as a result, an exceedingly great army arose. Interestingly, the word equipping is *"Katartismos* (Strong's #2677 meaning making fit, preparing, training, making fully qualified for service). In classical language the word is used for setting a bone during surgery; a recovered wholeness as when a broken limb is set and mends. It also means a 'discovered function' as when a physical member is properly operating."[5] Prophets in the body come and speak into things that are not operating as they ought.

Prophets are often seers. "The word *seer* is *roeh*, a visionary, one who sees visions. Roeh comes from the word *raah* which means to see but also has a wide range of meanings related to seeing (such as perceive, appear, discern, look, stare). It was only natural for Hebrew speakers to describe a prophet as a seer since prophets frequently received messages from God through visions."[6] Prophets see into the spiritual realm and often have discerning of spirits in their gift mix.

A good example in the Bible regarding the spiritual realm can be seen in the encounter of Elisha and his servant. The prophet prayed that his servant could see what he could see, and the Lord opened his eyes. He must have really been surprised when he saw such angelic support ready to fight on their behalf. He was surrounded by an angelic strike force. One can assume that this brought great comfort

---

5   Jack Hayford, *New Spirit-Filled Life Bible* (Nashville, TN: Thomas Nelson Inc., 2002), 1651.

6   Jack Hayford, *New Spirit-Filled Life Bible* (Nashville, TN: Thomas Nelson Inc.,2002), 371.

to Elisha's servant. Prophetic ministers look to relieve burdens and comfort the downcast.

> "Don't be afraid," the prophet answered. "Those who are with us are more than those who are with them." (Elisha saw in the spirit realm). And Elisha prayed, "Open his eyes, LORD, so that he may see." Then the LORD opened the servant's eyes, and he looked and saw the hills full of horses and chariots of fire all around Elisha. (2 Kings 6:16–17 NKJV)

Prophesying will come to convince and point you in the right direction. There was a time in Israel where there was no widespread revelation. The people were steeped in idolatry. The prophet Samuel comes on the scene, and none of his words fell to the ground (1 Samuel 3:19 NKJV). He spoke, and the people turned away from their idols. Not only that, the Philistines were subdued, and they did not come into the territory of Israel anymore (1 Sam.7:13 NKJV). The prophet can bring transformational power to change cities, regions, and nations.

Prophetic ministers often come with the counsel of the Lord. We see throughout the Old Testament prophets getting ahold of the Word of the Lord. They would then advise kings and military commanders.

Huldah, a prophetess in the reign of Josiah (2 Kings 22:14–20; 2 Chronicles 34:22–28), was sought out as she attested to the authenticity of the book of the law found by Hilkiah. She told the king what the Lord was going to do (bring ruin because the people were involved in idolatry). That very message influenced the king, and he brought change.

Interestingly, "Huldah's name means "to glide swiftly" (derived from the Hebrew root *cheled*). Her name may reflect her quickness of mind and her ability to swiftly and rightly discern the things of God. She had spiritual influence and was used to spark national revival."[7]

There are different spheres that God will call his prophetic ministers to implement change. Lance Wallnau speaks of seven different mountains of influence: they are education, religion, family, business, government/military, arts/entertainment, and media.[8] While there are opponents to his philosophy, one simply cannot deny that these systems exist, and we are to let our lights shine wherever we are.

Deborah's (the prophetess) main sphere was government. She was a judge over Israel and responsible to bring the counsel of the Lord. Her greatest characteristic was her courage and quick obedience to do what she heard from God. "She summoned Barak, the Israeli commander, to rally the troops for battle against insurmountable odds. She (Deborah) synchronized her life and actions with the time clock of heaven. The essence of the Deborah anointing is to understand that God has a calendar and that He has scheduled times for blessings, deliverance and even war."[9] Prophetic vessels are to be obedient and have full trust in the timing of the Lord to fulfill what He has spoken.

There were many male prophetic voices who brought the counsel of the Lord and even one who was greedy. His name was Balaam. For wages, he was willing to curse the people of God. The Bible tells us he was not able to do so. How many prophets today are peddling the Word of God for money? You should never have to pay to receive a word. Blessing a ministry is one thing, but putting a price on a word from the Lord is another. Rather recently, I had heard of a prophet asking to be paid for a "prophetic consultation." This was not "counseling." It was a promise to seek God for a word for your life and then come and give it to you at a cost.

---

[7] Jack Hayford, *New Spirit-Filled Life Bible* "The Woman and Todays Prophetic Possibilities (Huldah)" (Nashville: Thomas Nelson Inc., 2002), 512.

[8] GotQuestions.org, "What is the Seven Mountain Mandate? And is it Biblical?" Accessed 8/1/2020.

[9] Michele McClain Walters, *The Deborah Anointing* (Lake Mary, FL: Charisma House, 2015), 11.

This reminds me of the purchasing of indulgences in the eleventh and twelfth century. People would pay off the pope to remit their sins. The reason for the remembrance is twofold: (1) Man always wants to be in control; (2) Greed is involved.

The Bible is clear we cannot serve two masters. Prophets are to keep themselves pure and love God with their whole hearts. If mammon is their god, they have turned their backs on Jesus. This can happen. Judas was one of the apostles and sold out his Lord for thirty shekels. If self has become god, they have dethroned Christ off their hearts.

> Therefore, we must give the more earnest heed
> to the things we have learned, lest we drift away.
> (Hebrews 2:1 NKJV)

If you feel like you may have drifted in your walk and want to get your heart right, pray,

> *Father, I repent for allowing other things to take your place. I acknowledge that I am not on fire as I used to be. Fill me afresh today, Lord. In Jesus's name, amen.*

New Testament Prophetic Ministry

There is a prophet in the New Testament that intrigues me because she does not meet the full description or criteria we would consider to be a prophet. Her name is Anna the prophetess. There are no recorded prophecies, and she did not hold an office within the five-fold. First, let me say that some things do not always fit into our "theological containers" or nice little definitions or descriptions, but I do think it is important for you to know your kingdom assignment. Her story and assignment can be found in Luke 2:36–38.

If we look at her kingdom assignment, it may give us insight into her title—prophetess. Anna spent a great deal of time in the secret place. It is the place where it is between you and God. We know that Moses spoke to God face-to-face. God spoke to Moses frankly as a friend. It was a personal intimate relationship where there was an exchange of ideas and thoughts. Interestingly, the tent of meeting was called the bridal chamber. Prophets spend time in the secret place and minister unto God.

Anna, most likely, prayed for the coming Messiah and most likely declared messianic prophecies before the Lord. These declarations are prophetic acts. She agreed with the Word and would bring His word to remembrance. Anna knew her assignment was to pray in the Messiah. This is also known as prophetic intercession or praying in the will of the Lord.[10]

Today, we have the Holy Spirit in us, and He also comes upon us. Jesus sent the Holy Spirit to live in us, but there are times when

---

[10] James Goll. "The Art of Prophetic Intercession" God Encounter ministries.

His presence fills a room. You can feel the tangible weight of His glory. In any event, the Holy Spirit is here to help us with our intercession (Romans 26:8).

We should never assume that we know what God wants to do through our intercession. Jack Hayford tells us that "God may move through us with weeping, fastings, the gifts of the Holy Spirit, dreams, visions, mental pictures, impressions, verses of scriptures being quickened to us or silence?"[11] Silence? Yes. I have been in prayer services where a holy hush filled the room, and no one spoke. I have also been in prayer services where people would be overcome with weeping. We should always be open to the moving of the Holy Spirit who just might not move how you think He will.

If we look at the passage found in Isaiah 62:6–7, we can see prophetic intercession in all its beauty. They are watchmen crying out to God for His will to be performed. They do not stop praying until they see the Lord establish His will or promise.

> I have posted watchmen on your walls, Jerusalem they will never be silent day or night. You who call on the Lord, give yourselves no rest and give him no rest till he establishes Jerusalem and makes her the praise of the earth. (Isaiah 62:6–7 NIV)

Anna was a prophetic intercessor. She kept praying until she beheld the promised Messiah. Michele McClain Walters says, "When there is a set time to birth a promise of God on the earth, God drops a burden on a prophetic intercessor. It is a fusion of Gods revelation and insight into what needs to be prayed. God will direct you to pray to bring forth His will on the earth as it is in heaven." [12]

---

[11] Jack Hayford, *New Spirit-Filled Life Bible* (Nashville, TN: Thomas Nelson Inc., 2002), 1563.

[12] Michele McClain Walters, *The Anna Anointing* (Lake Mary, Fl: Charisma House, 2017), 43.

I believe the church has lost the art of travail. Many people shoot up popcorn prayers and go on their merry way. Sometimes you must give yourselves no rest or God no rest until he establishes the promise. In other words, you may have to war for your prophecies. Man always ought to pray and not lose heart (Luke 18:1).

Churches used to have shut-ins or all-night vigils praying until they had victory in certain areas. Did you know that there was "a prayer community organized in the 1700s in a part of Germany called Moravia? Known as the Moravians, they christened their community Hernhutt meaning 'The Lord's Watch.' The Lord's Watch established a 24-hour prayer vigil that lasted over 100 years."[13]

Anna spent her time with praying and fasting in the temple. She was believing to see the Messiah. God did not disappoint, and Jesus came right to her doorstep. She did not give up until she saw the promise fulfilled. She then testified about Jesus. Prophets will always point you to Jesus.

I mentioned a woman prophetess, but there were also men prophets in the New Testament. Jesus, John the Baptist, Judas, and Silas, Agabus, and John the Revelator are just a few. Whether male or female, God wants to speak to His people. He simply flows through different streams.

Various Prophetic Streams

Author James Goll brings some interesting insight into the different types of prophetic streams in his book: *The Seer*. He speaks of dreams, visions, prophetic intercessors, prophetic worshippers, and prophetic writers and counselors.[14] All of these avenues express God's heart in their own uniqueness. It is as a river making various streams to diffuse the glory of God.

---

[13] Jack Hayford, *New Spirit-Filled Life Bible* (Nashville, TN: Thomas Nelson Inc., 2002), 947.

[14] James W. Goll, *The Seer* (Shippensburg, PA: Destiny Publishers Inc., 2012), 43–50.

> There is a river whose streams shall make glad the
> city of God. (Psalm 46:4 NKJV)

I can also picture a diamond turning on a pivot, so you can behold another facet of God's splendor and manifold grace. Dr. Mike Bagwell refers to the word *manifold* in his article "1ˢᵗ Peter 4:10, "manifold."" He states, "Here is a corresponding (parallel) Greek word that thrills my soul. It is spelled 'poikilos,' and means 'diverse, variegated,' quite literally 'of various colors!'"[15] 1ˢᵗ Peter 4:9–10 is speaking of gifts given by God and our need to be good stewards of the manifold grace of God. In whatever way, God wants to speak to and through his vessels; it is all to be done for the glory of God.

> Each of you should use whatever gift you have
> received to serve others, as faithful stewards of
> God's grace in its various forms. If anyone speaks,
> they should do so as one who speaks the very
> words of God. If anyone serves, they should do
> so with the strength God provides, so that in all
> things God may be praised through Jesus Christ.
> To him be the glory and the power for ever and
> ever. Amen. (1 Peter 4:10–11 NIV)

One of the ways God speaks is through dreams. The Bible is replete with dreams and can be found in both Old and New Testaments. In the Old Testament, we see Joseph given dreams about his destiny, and King Nebuchadnezzar receiving dreams that troubled him (Daniel 2). In the New Testament, we read Joseph (who was betrothed to Mary) being visited by an angel in dreams.

It is interesting to note "the NT opens with a burst of dreams, visions, angelic visitations and prophecies and closes with John's revelation on the isle of Patmos. By citing so many significant examples it validates their existence and their use by God as a means of com-

---

[15] Dr. Mike Bagwell, 1ˢᵗ Peter 4:10, "manifold" (November 25, 2016), https://drmikebagwell.org/2016/11/25/1ˢᵗ-peter-410-manifold/.

municating hope."[16] These gifts from God are still manifesting today. Jesus is the same yesterday, today, and forever.

God also speaks in waking visions. Author James Goll points out the transfiguration on the Mount as an example.[17] This is where Jesus transfigures before Peter, James, and John, and they see Jesus talking to Elijah and Moses. They were then warned not to share the vision until the Son of Man was risen from the dead (Matthew 17:1–9).

This prophetic vision was incredibly significant as Jesus came to fulfil the law (Moses) and the prophets (Elijah) (see Matthew 5:17). It was a prophetic vision of what Jesus was about to fulfill upon His death on the cross and His resurrection. A new covenant would be "cut" not based on people fulfilling the external code of the Old Covenant (following the letter of the law), but Jesus Himself would lay down His life for our sins once and for all. He would then go to the Father and send the Holy Spirit.

The Holy Spirit will come into you as you receive Christ as your Lord and Savior. It is not by our works (following every law) but by grace through faith that we are saved. "The advantage of the New Covenant is that it is an inward power bearing the Spirit of God Himself, enabling us to keep God's law."[18]

The ability to keep every law was futile under the Mosaic law. The law showed us our need but was powerless to meet the need. Only the Spirit gives life.[19] The ministry of the Spirit is way more glorious.

> But if the ministry of death, written *and* engraved
> on stones, was glorious, so that the children of
> Israel could not look steadily at the face of Moses

---

[16] Jack Hayford, The *New Spirit-Filled Life Bible* (Nashville, TN: Thomas Nelson Inc., 2002), 1293.

[17] James W. Goll, *The Seer* (Shippensburg, PA: Destiny Image Publishers, Inc.2012), 70–82.

[18] Jack Hayford, The *New Spirit-Filled Life Bible* (Nashville, TN: Thomas Nelson Inc.), 1613.

[19] Ibid.

because of the glory of his countenance, which *glory* was passing away, how will the ministry of the Spirit not be more glorious? (2 Corinthians 3:7–8 NKJV)

The ministry of the Spirit enables sanctification, but other ministries of the Spirit is to speak to us, guide us into all truth, and show us things to come. One way the Spirit has spoken is through mental snapshots. The Holy Spirit would show me pictures of people who were about to come across my path and those who needed prayer. Once, I saw a friend reserving front row seats for me before I arrived at the assembly. Upon arrival, there she was waving me down to come to the front row. James Goll refers this type of vision as horasis. He says, "This occurs when the spirit who lives within us looks out through the windows of our eyes and allows us to see what he sees."[20]

Goll also refers to a vision called optasia, and the example he gives is seeing angels. [21] My daughter and I had a wonderful experience while viewing one of our church services online. We both saw a huge warrior-like angel with huge wings behind the pulpit and a smaller one with wings outlined with gold kneeling beside the pulpit. What made this experience extra odd was that when we went to watch again, there was nothing there. Another time, I saw a ball-like figure circling a young man's head. It then turned at me, and it had a skull face. The young man was very tormented and known to be very violent. So we see, there are good angels and demonic spirits in the spiritual realm.

One night during service, I fell into like a trancelike state. I looked up and saw the preacher. Around his head was a distinct ring of cloud. Some may call this a halo. Reported glory clouds and smoke have been seen by believers as well.

[20] James W. Goll, *The Seer* (Shippensburg, PA: Destiny Image Publishers Inc., 2012), 70–82.
[21] Ibid.

And the priests could not perform their service
because of the cloud, for the glory of the LORD
filled the temple of God. (2 Chronicles 5:14
NIV)

Prophetic songs have ministered to me as well as gifted counselors who had the wisdom of God in their toolbox. God has also spoken to me through life experiences, hearing other people's dialogues,
and yes, even license plates.

One day, while driving on the belt parkway in Brooklyn, I was
conversing with the Lord as to whether I should marry a particular man. I then said to the Lord: *He is not going to be my husband,
right?* At that very moment, a car drove by, and on its license plate,
it said, HE IS 2. Only God himself could have known what I was
asking at that moment, and only God could send that car at that
very moment. I am now happily married for twenty-one years to that
particular man.

Sometimes we think it must be a certain beak (a certain minister) that must feed us, but God can send any beak He wants to feed
or speak to His children. He sent a donkey to speak to Balaam and
John the Baptist (who wore camel hair and ate locusts) to prepare the
people for the way of the Lord. We also can get locked into a certain
way in which God will speak to us. It is time to take off the limita-
tions and be open to the manifold grace of God and the glorious
ministry of the Holy Spirit.

God most often speaks to me through the Scriptures and con-
firming His word by two or three witnesses. Dreams can sometimes
be wish fulfillment, and we know that man can deceive himself even
in the subconscious realm. This is not to say God does not give us
dreams or speak to us through them, but I do not believe they have
priority over God's written Word. Hopefully, the dream confirms the
Word whether it was *logos* or *rhema* (written or spoken respectively).

Your word *is* a lamp to my feet and a light to my
path. (Psalm 119:105 ESV)

Father, I pray to move more in the supernatural realm. I desire to have visions and dreams from You. I also desire to learn from you and want to study to show myself approved unto You. In Jesus's name, amen.

Testing the Word and Testing the Spirit

Many people have asked me, How are you certain if a prophecy is from God? My answer is, you must look at the message given and the messenger's beliefs. If they get Jesus wrong, everything else will be wrong. The Bible instructs us to test the spirits and points out if they do not confess, Jesus has come in the flesh is of God, then they are a false prophet. They must believe in the Virgin birth, the incarnation, and deity of Christ. They must also believe in the death, burial, and resurrection of Christ. If they have not confessed Jesus Christ is Lord of all, they are not saved.

> Beloved, believe not every spirit, but try the spirits whether they are of God: because many false prophets are gone out into the world. Hereby know ye the Spirit of God: Every spirit that confesseth that Jesus Christ is come in the flesh is of God. (1 John 4:1–2 KJV)

Many cults fall short in this area. They get Jesus wrong altogether. They are deceived.

Examine the Word

The prophetic word must also be examined. It must be held up to the light of God's Word. One must ask, Is the message contrary to God's Word and overall precepts found in the Holy Writ? For example, God is not going to tell you that someone else's husband is for you. This is coming from the soul realm. God's system of morality and holy conduct is in the life manual we call the Bible. There is safety in staying in the confines of God's Word. Another example may be someone saying the Lord told them the date of His return. Well, the Bible is clear: no one knows the hour, only the Father.

> But about that day or hour no one knows, not even the angels in heaven, nor the Son but only the Father. (Mark 13:32 NKJV)

Examine How You Felt After Receiving the Word

The next litmus test is, is the word pure, peaceable, and easy to entreat? Do you walk away feeling condemned with no hope of redemption? James 3:17 tells us, "But the wisdom that is from above is first pure, then peaceable, gentle, willing to yield, full of mercy and good fruits, without partiality and without hypocrisy."

With that said, did you walk away feeling ashamed or judged? Prophecy should have a redeeming quality about it. Sometimes people come and attempt to put word curses on the people of God. Those curses, however, cannot alight without a cause, but you can feel their impact. The Bible is clear that death and life are in the power of tongue. We can use our tongues to bless and at times to curse. The tongue can be an unruly evil. As Christians, our conversations should be imparting grace.

I heard of a minister getting a word to get his house in order, for there was not much time left. He was afraid in his heart for three days until he realized it was a word curse. Interestingly, I warned him about that person, and that warning was quickened to him by the Spirit. He then felt very relieved. I had heard this "prophet" prophesy in prior meetings, and my spirit just did not bear witness.

Does Your Spirit Bear Witness?

Does your spirit bear witness to the Word being spoken over you? You spirit will bear witness to the truth. Peace is an indicator that God is behind what is being spoken. Conversely, confusion is from the evil one. I would say let the peace of God be the umpire of your heart. Let it call the shots.

I personally get what they call a "check" in the spirit. Something just does not seem right to me when a prophecy is off or a teaching has some slight doctrinal error. It is like I feel a clunk in my spirit man, an alert goes off. I once got prophesied over by someone, and I walked away feeling incredibly angry. Frankly, I do not remember what was spoken, but what I remember about this man was he always seemed angry and agitated. He tried to transfer his own anger on to me. Perhaps that lessened the intensity of anger he had. I believe he was quickly divorced after that. *Hmm?*

I have learned to listen and rely on checks in the spirit. They tell me when God is not in something, or they are saying wait on the Lord. I have learned not to override a check even when things seemed so good. This can be likened to running through red lights. There will be consequences for disobeying the Spirit. Sometimes we override checks in the Spirit because we want something bad. I, at that point, must check why I am not content with what I have and perhaps look at covetousness. I have learned to examine myself and ask God to search my heart.

Examine Content and Flow of the Word

Prophets who judge a word also look at the content and flow of the prophetic word. Questions such as, Is it making sense, and is the person continually stopping to think about what to add on? The word prophecy means to bubble forth (like a spring). A spring has a flow. Prophetic utterances flow.

Sometimes people just want to be heard and will step out and just say anything. Leaders must be careful with this. The enemy knows what to do to disrupt a prophetic flow. Other times, a person may have felt the prophetic anointing, so they thought it was their turn to speak out.

As a young Christian, God once gave me a prophetic tongue to utter. It was a beautiful experience. I felt liquid love pour out all over me, and then I spoke in a beautiful language I knew not of, and it was interpreted. But whenever I felt the anointing, I thought I had to speak out in tongues (loud). What I ended up doing was disrupting the service. The pastor gently brought correction in private. I was really embarrassed. So I do understand the awkwardness of moving in the spirit.

Is It Timely? Does It Gel?

Prophetic words are timely and relevant. The Holy Spirit is not confused and will distribute the gift of prophecy to help meet needs in the congregation. He will look to build, comfort, and console. I have found a profound insensitivity to the spirit of God in many churches. This has been evidenced by scrolling on Facebook during service, having loud conversations while an altar call is going, or blurting out left field prophecies. An example of this would be declaring gloom and doom when we are in the presence of *joy* or, conversely, laughing during a somber moment. This in part, I believe, is because many of God's people are not really spending time with Him. It is in their own prayer closets where sensitivity is developed to atmospheres and *His voice*.

I think the tone of the word really needs to be looked at as well. Is it angry? Is it negative? We are to speak the truth in love. There was once a woman in the church who would yell at the people. The sheep were afraid of her. The pastor had to bring gentle correction. She left the church and, of course, spoke badly about the pastors on the way out.

It is particularly important to examine the spirit behind what is being said. The soul sometimes leaks, especially if there are untreated wounds. If the person has been very wounded, he may have evil suspicions which clouds the ability to discern. If they have envy in their heart, this opens the door for the evil one to operate. For where there is envy and strife, there is confusion and every evil work (James 3:16 KJV).

If trauma has left the person feeling insecure, they may open the door to Jezebel for feelings of power. If they are feeling insignificant, they may open the door to Ahab. When this happens, the individual may simply comply to any power perceived to be stronger than himself. If they have unresolved anger, this will come out in their prophetic stream, and people will automatically shut down and not receive. If they feel depressed, they can release depression into the atmosphere and cause a transference of spirit. Prophets are to be atmosphere changers.

Timing of a word is crucial in services. God has spent time preparing the hearts to receive, and then at the right time, he drops the prophetic seed into the ground of the heart. The enemy will know exactly when to use a person to bring the service into another direction. I have seen worship teams not stopping for the word to be released, and I have heard demonic shrieks go forth under a heavy anointing.

If it is disruptive, the person is out of order. God is a God of order. True prophetic vessels have great respect for the order of God and get agitated when things get out of alignment.

Look at the Messenger

What do you discern about the person delivering? It is important that a person speaking for God is not looking for personal recognition. This will manifest with a haughty spirit. We must guard the anointing. God resists the proud but gives grace to the humble. A person who self-exalts is not exalting Jesus and unfortunately is very immature. He is still a babe. He is still carnal.

We must look at the life of the person. This goes for every area of ministry. Is he a good husband? Does she takes care of her children? Is there a love for money?

> Wherefore by their fruits ye shall know them.
> (Matthew 7:20 KJV)

The Bible is clear that we know them by their fruits, not the gifts. Please remember, babes can move in gifts, but fruit takes time to be cultivated. Also, gifting and callings are irrevocable. So the person may have gotten saved ten years ago, moved mightily in the spirit, and knew he was called but chose to go out in the world. This person may move in a gift, but his character needs development. People with bad character often disable their hearers.

We also need to ask, What is the fruit of their relationship with God? Is the person loving? Does he have joy and peace? Is he faithful and exercising self-control? Or is he lawless and unable to be taught?

I know, personally, I would have a great deal of trouble receiving from someone who was not open to receiving correction from leadership. Pride is evident.

> But the fruit of the Spirit is love, joy, peace, forbearance, kindness, goodness, faithfulness, gentleness and self-control. Against such things there is no law. (Galatians 5:22–23 NIV)

Another point to look at is, What is the fruit of their ministry? Does this ministry manifest in the demonstration of the spirit and power? Are their words flat, general, and have no weight to it? A man or woman who spends time seeking the Lord with their whole hearts come with a "tangible weight" and is not found wanting.

Prophetic words need to be judged and examined carefully. To "judge a word (diakrino) can mean to separate thoroughly and implies the ability to dissect what was spoken and see if it is a correct statement. The Greek word *krino* is a legal term meaning to make a decision on the basis of the information presented, similar to the informed decision a jury makes after hearing the pertinent information."[22]

---

[22] Perry Stone, "How to Judge a Prophetic Word," Ministrytodaymag.com.

> Do not despise prophetic utterances but examine everything carefully. (1 Thessalonians 5:20–21 NASB)

You know where it says *Mene tekel, upharsin, Tekel* means "you have been weighed on the scales and found deficient" (Daniel 5:27).

Two or three prophets should speak, and the other should weigh carefully what is said (1 Corinthians 14:29).

I want to share that some are still yet immature, and sometimes they are not sensitive to the delivery time or the mood of God, and some are not able to discern whether it is for them personally or a corporate word.

One time, a man heard the Lord say to him, *Stop looking at all the pretty girls; look to Me.* He prophesied this word to the congregation. I have found being around other prophetic voices will sharpen you. It will bring accountability and wisdom.

I think it is crucial to see if the message looks to exalt Jesus or the prophet! I also think that believers need to know the Word for themselves. If a believer truly spends time in the Word, he will be able to spot the genuine from a fake. Just like a bank teller who deals with real money all day knows when a fake bill passes her hand. We need to spend time with the genuine to spot the fake.

Finally, I want to issue a warning about arrogant prophets not connected with any members in the body of Christ. If they present a "better than you" presentation and make you feel less than, I would be careful about what I receive from them. Jesus never modeled this type of superiority. God detests a haughty spirit (Proverbs 6:1).

Also, beware of rogue prophets that are not connected to any local assembly. Some of these rogues were hurt by the church, set off on their own, and now carry an anti-church spirit.

I went to a meeting one time. There was about twenty people in attendance. One after another, they began to share how terrible the church was to them. You could feel the disdain in the room. I left that meeting feeling very grieved. Jesus was not lifted up.

An anti-church spirit has risen in some gatherings. You can sometimes find it in small home groups where a few disgruntled members of a church split off to start a new work. Unfortunately, it is not likely that the blessing of the Lord will be upon this new adventure. Their hearts are not right before the Lord. They have forgotten that Christ laid down his life for the church. He loves his bride. They have also forgotten that Jesus declared in His Word that He would build His church, and the gates of hell will not prevail against it.

> *Father, I pray you would help me be more sensitive to the moving of your Spirit. I ask for increased discernment. In Jesus's name.*

Accurately Representing the King and the Kingdom

True prophetic ministers have a heart of compassion for the people they minister to. Their compassion has mostly been birthed out of brokenness. For as the sufferings of Christ abound in us, so our consolation also abounds through Christ (2 Corinthians 1:5 NKJV).

> God comforts us in all our troubles so we can comfort those in any trouble with the comfort we ourselves receive from God. (2 Corinthians 1:4 NIV)

Any minister that has not really gone through suffering cannot effectively aid another in their suffering. You want a minister with some battle scars—one who can navigate you through some battles.

Most prophets I know have gone through major wars, and because of them, he or she can bring great consolation. Author John Parsons, *Hebrews for Christians*, stated, "Only when we realized our powerlessness and radical insufficiency can we come to know Yeshua as *Moshia*, as our savior. And this is the ongoing state of dependency, we walk with a limp as did Israel."[23]

Prophetic ministers want to see Christ formed in you. They are not intimidated by your gift and want to see you excel. If there

---

[23] John Parson, *The Beautitudes of Jesus*, www.hebrew4christians.com

43

is jealousy, they are not yet perfected in love. They are still afraid of being replaced by someone else and not yet developed or matured in Father's love. Perfect love will cast out all fear.

Joseph's brothers were jealous of Joseph because of their father's favor toward him. This was truly evidenced when their father adorned only Joseph with a coat of many colors. Our heavenly Father shows no partiality. He does not have favorites, but He does have intimates. In other words, if you are saved, you can have as much of God as you like.

As God's ministers and spokespersons, we do the work of an ambassador. Author David Paul Tripp says, "Living a representative lifestyle can be summarized by three points of focus: the message of the king, the method of the king, and the *character of the king*." [24]

The Message of the King

As an ambassador, I want to communicate any message from the King accurately. If someone is not saved, the good news of Jesus Christ (the King of glory) must be presented (see John 3:16; 1 Corinthians 15:3–4; Romans 10:9–10). If someone is saved, any prophetic word must be aligned with God's Word and overall benevolence.

> But the wisdom that comes from heaven is first of all pure; then peace-loving, considerate, submissive, full of mercy and good fruit, impartial and sincere. (James 3:17 NIV)

The wisdom of God is not tainted nor is it strife stirring, rude, or bias. It is not full of harsh judgment but rather full of compassion and fruit bearing. The intent of the wisdom is always for our good.

---

[24] Paul David Tripp, *Instruments in the Redeemer's Hands* (Phillipsburg, NJ: P&R Publishing, 2002), 107.

The Method of the King

Our King is full of loving-kindness and speaks the truth in love. Our method should be the same. Christ is tenderhearted and forgiving; we should be to. Jesus was meek and lowly at heart. He tells us to learn from Him (Matthew 11:29 NKJV). Apostle Paul said to imitate him as he imitated Christ (see 1 Corinthians 11:1 NKJV).

It must also be pointed out, however, that our King Jesus did, at times, confront unrighteousness. There are times when a righteous indignation will rise within us, and we must confront evil. Our silence could be seen as collusion. I do believe that, at times, the church has been sleeping when it should have been confronting the evils of society.

The Character of the King

We know that God is motivated by love. His character is one of humility. We too must clothe ourselves with humility and be dispensers of His love. Abrasive prophetic ministers who are harsh are not accurately representing the method or character of the King. Prophetic ministers are to bring encouragement, exhortation, and consolation (1 Corinthians 14:3), and they are to speak the truth in love (Ephesians 4:15).

> But the one who prophesies speaks to people for their strengthening, encouraging and comfort. (1 Corinthians 14:3 NIV)

> Instead, speaking the truth in love, we will grow to become in every respect the mature body of him who is the head, that is, Christ. (Ephesians 4:15 NIV)

Character development is crucial if any minister wants to be effective. Jesus warned of hypocrisy. Ministers cannot tell someone to do something and then turn around and not do it themselves. Jesus rebuked the scribes and Pharisees for it.

> So you must be careful to do everything they tell you. But do not do what they do, for they do not practice what they preach. They tie up heavy, cumbersome loads and put them on other people's shoulders, but they themselves are not willing to lift a finger to move them. (Matthew 23:3–4 NIV)

Ministers must be on time for their meetings, keep their word, and have a lifestyle above reproach. They avoid even the appearance of evil. They keep themselves pure. They watch over their words.

The tongue of the righteous is choice silver (Prov.10:20 NKJV), and the righteous study how to answer (Prov. 15:28 NKJV). They are not impulsive as impulsivity impulsivity exalts folly (Prov.14:29 NKJV). Ministers keep their word even until it hurts (Psalm 15:4).

Prophets are schooled in the Word. They have studied to show themselves approved unto God. How will they encourage if they have *no* Word in them?

I once knew a woman who thought it was her job (she believed herself to be a prophet and goes by that title) to tell everybody their weakness and even blast people on Facebook. The Bible is clear if she had a problem with someone, she is to go to them first, so clearly, she was in error and does not know the Word.

These people are called bone pickers. They do not have Father's heart. They have a religious demon. Remember, anyone can point out a weakness. Love looks to cover a multitude of sins. Two of Noah's sons walked backward into the tent to cover their father's nakedness.

Prophets move in meekness which is exercising God's strength under His control. They represent the kingdom and release the power of God.

> For the kingdom of God is not a matter of talk but of power. (1 Corinthians 4:20 NLT)

> It is not meat or drink but righteousness, peace,
> and joy in the Holy Ghost. (Romans 4:17 KJV)

Many supposed prophets have given extremely general words that can apply to anyone (i.e., God is going to use you). Really? I have also seen some say the same exact word over everybody, every time.

I was once in a congregation where I saw some visiting prophets. Something in my heart was not right, so I started to fast and pray. That very week, one of the prophets was exposed as a false prophet. He told a woman to leave her husband because he was not super spiritual. She was a *beautiful* woman. You get where I am going.

Discerning of Spirits

There is general discernment which is a product of living on the planet for a while and study, and then there is the gift of discerning of spirits that comes from the Holy Spirit.

Discerning of spirits goes beyond our natural abilities and only God can impart.[25] Derek Prince says the discerning of spirits is the supernatural ability to recognize and distinguish between not only good and bad but various classes of spirit. The classes are the Holy Spirit, good angels, demon spirits, the human spirit. [26]

Another definition is a supernatural perception for the purpose of determining the source of spiritual activity (John Wimber). [27] Francis Frangipane calls it the grace to see into the unseen.[28]

Some have reported smelling the presence of the Lord as lilacs or roses. Others in the deliverance ministry have reported smelling bad cheese or sulfur when unclean spirits were present.

---

[25] James W. Goll, *The Seer* (Shippensburg, PA: Destiny Publishers Inc., 2012), 106.
[26] James W. Goll, *The Seer* (Shippensburg, P.A: Destiny Publishers Inc.), 106.
[27] Ibid., 107
[28] Ibid., 108

47

Some have seen angels or glory clouds in the room. Sometimes people have felt pain particularly in the areas where he wants to release physical healing.

The gift of discernment comes to show you what you are dealing with in deliverance and the area of error. The gift of discernment will allow you to see if someone is genuine or after money. The gift of the discernment will also show you a haughty spirit.

In these last days, we must have the gift of discernment in full operation. There are many charlatans looking to make money off the naïve. There are also people looking for power as well. Their service is coming from a heart of covetousness. We must have the gift to target these problems before they cause division in the body.

My Spiritual Experiences

Recently, I went to Indiana, and I felt blasted with God's glory before a meeting. I went outside, and the people who were with me said, "Pastor, there is gold dust all over your face." It was real, but, of course, I went to check my make up to see if it had any sparkles.

Another time, I went to Dr. Carol Elaine's meeting, and I looked at my hands, and there were gold specks. I dismissed it as hand lotion. My girlfriend called me the next day and said, "Hey, did you get the gold dust last night?"

I once saw a goiter shrink to nothing and a woman healed of brain cancer after the laying on of hands. God moves in the supernatural realm. There will always be doubters.

People came to me and said the gold was phooey and not of God. They called it a lying sign and wonder and not found in the Bible. I had to disagree as the streets of heaven are paved with gold, and I am seated in heavenly places, and my citizenship is in heaven (Philippians 3:20). Finding some gold on me does not seem too far-fetched.

I have seen the "evil eye," and people walking around stealthy like to come and check out our services. God does and will show you their heart by their eyes, how they carry themselves, and their words. God will show you the intent and motives of hearts.

Attacks Against the Prophetic Ministers

First, I want to say the enemy despises all those who represent the King and the kingdom. It is important to note that it is the Christ in you (the hope of glory) Satan wants to destroy. He comes to rob, kill, and destroy.

If you are not solidified in who you are in Christ, you will shrink back. Therefore, it is so important that we grasp the identification theology Dr. Jerry Brandt speaks of.

1. The Kingdom of God is now present with all the authority and power of Jesus Christ and is available to the church.
2. Identification theology is based on revelation of what God says about who we are.
3. We are to function under His authority as kings and priests unto our God.
4. It is a deeper look at who Christ is and who we are declared to be now in light of his nature and existence.[29]

We hear in Matthew 3:17 when God says, "This is My beloved Son in whom I am well-pleased." God clearly declares Jesus as His Son; He says He is loved. So the good Father brings affirmation of his love and identity. Satan, the father of lies, attacks these two basic foundations. If you are the son of God (attack on identity), prove who you are. Jump off the cliff is saying, let Father prove His love by

---

[29] Jerry Brandt, *I Am who you Say I Am* (Tampa, FL: Jerry Brandt, 2019), 81.

catching you. Jesus answers the attack of Satan with the word—*it is written.*

Even in the garden, the serpent comes and says, "Did God really say you shall not eat of the fruit?" What was Satan doing? He was trying to show them that God was withholding and, perhaps, really did not love them like they thought?

We must know who we are in our God and become perfected in His love as manifested sons and daughters. Spirit-filled believers have power to change atmospheres as they have the same spirit in them that raised Christ from the dead, darkness to light in a moment's time.

Jentezen Franklin notes,

> It is important to understand atmospheres and your ability to change them because Jesus has authorized and empowered you to do so. I have heard it said that Christians are not to be spiritual thermometers but spiritual thermostats. In other words, you are not merely supposed to detect the spiritual climate as a thermometer detects the existing temperature in a room; you are to change it, imposing the authority of the Kingdom of God wherever you go.[30]
>
> Satan will resist exposure and will resist anyone who attempts to bring the light of God upon their hidden works.[31]

In the book of Acts, we can clearly see resistance to Apostle Paul. He comes up against a spirit of divination as he and others are on their way to prayer.

---

[30] Jentezen Franklin, *The Spirit of Python* (Lake Mary, FL: Charisma House, 2013), 41.
[31] Jentezen Franklin, *The Spirit of Python* (Lake Mary, FL: Charisma House, 2013), 39.

> Once when we were going to the place of prayer, we were met by a female slave who had a spirit by which she predicted the future. She earned a great deal of money for her owners by fortune-telling. She followed Paul and the rest of us, shouting, "These men are servants of the Most High God, who are telling you the way to be saved." She kept this up for many days. Finally, Paul became so annoyed that he turned around and said to the spirit, "In the name of Jesus Christ I command you to come out of her!" At that moment, the spirit left her. (Acts 16:16–18 NIV)

Paul knew it was a different spirit even though the woman was saying the right things. Prophetic often comes with discernment.

Satan likes to counterfeit the things of God. Fortune-telling is a counterfeit. He uses the hunger for the supernatural and traps people in his web. It is a distraction to keep people from seeking the true supernatural realm that God moves in. In this case, distraction was being used to detour Paul and the rest from preaching the good news. I would suggest not only to listen to what is being said but also the spirit behind what is being said.

Other attacks ministers encounter is from religious folks. Cessationists have attacked the prophetic by saying the gifts are not for today. Religious spirits have a mindset that will not be changed (staunch). They will never desire the new wine. They really do not know Jesus.

> Search the scriptures; for in them ye think ye have eternal life: and they are they which testify of me. And ye will not come to me, that ye might have life. (John 5:39–40 KJV)

Now I will talk about the Jezebel spirit. We read about her as the wicked queen who kills the prophets in the Old Testament. That spirit has taken up residence in some humans. It is a devious and manipulative spirit that always wants control. It uses seduction and can be relentless until it achieves its goal. The goal is to kill the prophetic gift. The spirit wants to remain hiding and not to be exposed to the light. It uses masquerading and other various tricks to keep people blinded to what is going on.

I have encountered this spirit several times in ministry. It is very sneaky. It first tries to get very close to leadership. It likes to be around the true anointing to obtain credibility. It flatters you and wants to know all about you under the guise of care. It wants to learn everything about you, especially weaknesses. This is so it can be used as a manipulative card down the road. Your words will be twisted always to the spirit's advantage. It changes the rules as you play the game, and it holds the rule book. Author Steve Sampson in his book *Confronting Jezebel* speaks of how the Jezebel spirit likes to sequester information to control the flow of information and use it as leverage.[32]

One minute, you will feel sorry for it, and the next, you will feel provoked. You will begin to feel like you have no confidence in your prophetic gifting. You will find yourself questioning everything about your ministry.

This spirit will discredit all those close to you and you will find yourself becoming very suspicious. I personally wondered if I had any friends left in the ministry. The person with the Jezebel spirit seemed to be my only true friend. I found myself saying yes to things that were really a *no* in my heart. You will feel like you are always doing something wrong when you are doing everything by the book.

The Jezebel spirit claims to be prophetic as well, but it is most likely that she/he is only remarkably high in emotional intelligence. By this, I mean they can read people and know their weaknesses. This is not prophetic. This spirit knows how to pull on your heartstrings to get its demands met. Samspon adds, the Jezebel spirits operates in clairvoyance and mysticism.[33]

---

[32] Steve Sampson. Confronting Jezebel: Discerning and Defeating the Spirit of Control. (Bloomington MN: Chosen Books, 2012),84
[33] Ibid. 86

This spirit is extremely jealous and looks to kill through character assassination. This spirit is a human cannibal. It will leave you feeling pitiful like a worm for even questioning what she does or does not do. You will get knots in your stomach when dealing with this spirit. It wants to destroy your ministry. You cannot allow it to. You must guard your lentil patch! This spirit wants to make an Ahab out of you.

To counteract a Jezebel, let us look at the actions of Jehu in 2 Kings 9:36–37 NIV:

> Then Jehu went to Jezreel. When Jezebel heard about it, she put on eye makeup, arranged her hair, and looked out of a window. As Jehu entered the gate, she asked, "Have you come in peace, you Zimri, you murderer of your master?"
>
> He looked up at the window and called out, "Who is on my side? Who?" Two or three eunuchs looked down at him. "Throw her down!" Jehu said. So, they threw her down, and some of her blood spattered the wall and the horses as they trampled her underfoot.
>
> Jehu went in and ate and drank. "Take care of that cursed woman," he said, "and bury her, for she was a king's daughter." But when they went out to bury her, they found nothing except her skull, her feet and her hands. They went back and told Jehu, who said, "This is the word of the LORD that he spoke through his servant Elijah the Tishbite: On the plot of ground at Jezreel dogs will devour Jezebel's flesh. Jezebel's body will be like dung on the ground in the plot at Jezreel, so that no one will be able to say, 'This is Jezebel.'"

Jehu was on a God-given mission. He would not allow anything to deter him from his mission. He was focused and drove furiously to fulfill it. He ran with aim, not as one flailing his arms in the air. He certainly was no shadow boxer.

We read in scripture that Jezebel put on eye makeup and arranged her hair. She hoped to use her charm and seduction with Jehu but to no avail. Her eye makeup and arranged hair could not seduce Jehu. She then tries provocative questioning, but Jehu has no dialogue with her. He refuses to get entrapped by her cunning. The story of Jezebel ends when the eunuchs throw her down the wall, and then the horses trample her underfoot, and the dogs eat her.

This reminds me of "demolishing strongholds" and destroying yokes by reason of the anointing. Jehu was packing with a commander anointing and fulfilled his mission.

I believe God is raising up mighty warriors in these last days. They will not tolerate any injustice. They will fight for that which is right in the sight of their God.

They will take a stand against evil and the workers of iniquity. Their only desire is to please the commander who enlisted them: Jesus. These ministers will be a voice for the voiceless and relieve the oppressed. They will love their God and walk humbly before Him.

They are uncompromisable and will not bow to this world system. They are courageous and will roar the Word of the Lord. These firebrands will stand in any fiery affliction and not back down to pressure.

God is doing a new thing, and now, it shall bring forth. Shall ye not perceive it? (see Isa. 43:19)

False Prophets and Discerning the Voice of God

The Bible tells us that we will know false prophets by their fruit, not by their gifts. Many are bedazzled by charisma and make quick assessments. We are instructed to look at the fruit of the person. The Bible also tells us his speech will reveal what is in his heart.

> Beware of the false prophets, who come to you in sheep's clothing, but inwardly are ravenous wolves. You will know them by their fruits. Grapes are not gathered from thorn *bushes* nor figs from thistles, are they? So every good tree bears good fruit, but the bad tree bears bad fruit. A good tree cannot produce bad fruit, nor can a bad tree produce good fruit. Every tree that does not bear good fruit is cut down and thrown into the fire. So then, you will know them by their fruits. (Matthew 7:15–20 NKJV)

> The good man out of the good treasure of his heart brings forth what is good; and the evil *man* out of the evil *treasure* brings forth what is evil; for his mouth speaks from that which fills his heart. (Luke 6:45 NASB)

Over time, you will hear the heart of a false prophet. They outwardly look like sheep, but inwardly, they are ravenous wolves ready to pounce. Many of them are using ministry only for monetary gain and have fallen into the error of Balaam.

> Woe to them! For they have gone in the way of
> Cain, have run greedily in the error of Balaam
> for profit, and perished in the rebellion of Korah.
> (Jude 1:11 NKJV)

False prophets speak contrary to the teachings of Jesus. They may deny that Christ came in the flesh (1 John 4:2–3), disguise themselves as an angel of light (2 Corinthians 11:14), and even use flattery to win the people over (see Romans 16:18).

> This is how you can recognize the Spirit of God:
> Every spirit that acknowledges that Jesus Christ
> has come in the flesh is from God, but every spirit
> that does not acknowledge Jesus is not from God.
> This is the spirit of the antichrist, which you have
> heard is coming and even now is already in the
> world. (1 John 4:2–3 NIV)

> Satan himself transforms himself into an angel of
> light. (2 Corinthians 11:14 NKJV)

> For they that are such serve not our Lord Jesus
> Christ, but their own belly; and by good words
> and fair speeches deceive the hearts of the simple.
> (Romans 16:18 KJV)

We must look at the fruit they are producing. In other words, does their teaching have any godly impact on their followers? Are their followers chasing after purity and righteousness?

It would be wise to really study the content of the preacher's message as well as the intent of his heart. Does he exalt Jesus who is full of grace and truth, or does he try to put you back under the *law*? Does he show genuine care for the sheep or simply dismiss them?

Most examples of spiritual abuse refer to a church elder or faith leader inflicting abuse on congregation members often by creating a toxic culture within the church or group by shaming or controlling members using the power of their position.[34] A common characteristic of an abusive religious system is that the real needs of the people are not met. The sheep are not genuinely cared for.

I also think it is important to take note if the preacher comes with some "new revelation" that no one has heard of. Apostle Paul said even if an angel of heaven comes with a different gospel, let him be accursed (Galatians 1:8).

A true prophetic minister has very distinct markers. For one, they are extremely sensitive to injustice and are often a voice for those who cannot speak up for themselves. They look to relieve the oppressed and set people free.

They are very alert to doctrinal error and despise idols. We know that Apostle Paul was greatly disturbed when he saw a city full of idol worship. The true prophetic looks to tear down idols and restore worship in the house of God.

Finally, the true prophetic minister pursues righteousness, peace, and gentleness. They are on a godly pursuit and encourage others to do so. Being very keen in the spirit, they know when things are out of order.

Is That You, Lord?

I want to talk about how you know something is from God and give you some tools to increase your sensitivity to His voice.

First, I want to say we all have missed it on occasion. We may have misinterpreted what He said; we may have been unclear to what has been said, or we may have even dismissed it because it seemed ridiculous.

---

[34] Spiritual Abuse, Hotline.org.

Sometimes you think it is just your thoughts, but it was God speaking to you. Sometimes it is just an exceptionally light impression or a mental picture. Samuel, as a young lad, heard a voice speaking but thought it was Eli calling him. He eventually perceived the voice of the Lord. I believe over time, you will quickly recognize the voice of God. God's sheep hear His voice.

God is speaking continuously through His Word, through our circumstances, through other believers, through dreams and visions. We just need to become more focused or "incline our ears." The word *incline* means "willing, ready, prepared, pitch, lean into, ascent."

I am talking about spiritual ears, although God has been known to speak audibly on occasion. We must first draw nigh to God, and He will draw nigh to us.

Second, tuning out distractions and disciplining ourselves to sit quietly before the Lord is a must. Submission, solitude, and silence are spiritual channels of grace.

God often speaks to people through their spirits. When I read the Word, scriptures are "quickened" to me. They are illuminated by the Holy Spirit and literally come alive or jump in my spirit. Other times, it simply is a *knowing* that God is sharing with me. This is the still small voice.

James 3:17, I believe, is one of the best scriptures to tell us if a word is from God: "But the wisdom that is from above is first pure, then peaceable, gentle, *and* easy to be intreated, full of mercy and good fruits, without partiality, and without hypocrisy."

So conversely, we can say if what is speaking is tainted, agitating, rough, hard to swallow, lacking compassion, bias, and self-agenda driven, we can conclude it is not from God.

Jesus said to come to Him, and He would give us rest. The Word will bring you rest, a comfort. So when seeking the Lord about something, do you have a rest in your spirit, or do you have a resting place? Have the soles of your feet found a resting place? In Genesis 8:9, the dove could not find a resting place; she returned to the ark. Some of us simply need to return to the ark.

Conclusion

The Bible tells us to eagerly desire to prophesy, for it brings edification to the body. It is a desire for a good work. God wants to flow through his honorable vessels and be a continual blessing here on the earth. He is a good God and is determined to do good. His spoken and written Word continually brings forth life. The prophetic speaks life to the dead, and it can come alive.

Without the prophetic ministry in operation, things will go awry. Hope will be hindered. Despair will creep in. Prophetic writers, psalmists, and counselors will go to the grave and people will have been robbed of the blessing of their gifts. What a shame that would be.

I wholeheartedly believe that the prophetic ministry is so under attack because of its ability to bring forth life and evoke hope. It is inspirational and encouraging. And while it has come up against major attacks, I believe God is restoring honor to it.

The ministry of the prophet is vital to bring the body to a higher level of maturity. This leadership office also helps guide and govern the ship. Prophets need to be at the helm with the apostles to avoid shipwreck. The body needs their governance, equipping, and nurturing "till we all come to the unity of the faith and of the knowledge of the Son of God, to a perfect man, to the measure of the stature of the fullness of Christ" (Ephesians 4:13 NKJV).

I do believe that God wants us to be successful and delights to reveal secrets to us. He does, however, want a more intimate walk with each one of us. We simply need to draw nigh unto Him. The Bible tells us to call unto Him, and He will answer us and show us mighty things we do not yet know (see Jeremiah 33:3).

It all starts with knowing Jesus. If you do not know Jesus as your Lord and Savior and would like to, please pray the following:

> *I believe Jesus, the Son of God, died on the cross for my sins and rose from the dead. He is the only acceptable sacrifice for my sins. Jesus, please forgive me of all my sins and be Lord over my life. Come into my heart. You alone are my Savior. In Jesus's name, amen.*

If you prayed this prayer from your heart, you are now born-again. Welcome to the family of God.

Find a good, spirit-filled, bible-believing church and bloom where the Lord has planted you. Be obedient and serve. This is the greatest honor of all.

Bibliography

Books

Brandt, Jerry. *I Am who you say I Am: Believe it! Declare It!* Tampa, FL: Jerry Brandt, 2019.

Franklin, Jentezen. *The Spirit of Python.* Lake Mary, FL: Charisma House, 2013.

Goll, James. *The Seer: The Prophetic Power of Visions, Dreams and Open Heavens.* Shippensburg, PA: Destiny Image, 2012.

Hayford, Jack. Word Wealth. *New Spirit-Filled Life Bible.* 2002.

Sampson, Steve. *Confronting Jezebel: Discerning and Defeating the Spirit of Control.* Bloomington, MN: Chosen Books, 2012.

Tripp, Paul David. *Instruments in the Redeemer's Hands.* Philipsburg NJ: P&R Publishing, 2002.

Walters, Michelle McClain. *The Anna Anointing.* Lake Mary, FL: Charisma House, 2017.

Internet

Goll, James. "The art of Prophetic Intercession" God Encounter Ministries.

Parker, Joseph. *The People's Bible: Discourses on Holy Scripture,* "Prophets and Builders." Ezra v, vi. p.172.

Parsons, John. "The Beautitudes of Jesus." www.hebrew4christians.com.

Pattico, Stuart. "The Difference Between the Gift of Prophecy and the Office of the Prophet." www.stuartpattico.com. April 2017.

Spiritual Abuse. Hotline.org.

Stone, Perry. "How to Judge a Prophetic Word." Ministrytoday-mag.com.

About the Author

April Griseta is a doctor of ministry and holds a license to practice mental health counseling. She also copastors New and Lively Hope Ministries with her husband Joe. April is a sought out national conference speaker and hosts the popular TV program *Bounce Back* on Christian Television Network. She has moved in both the prophetic and deliverance ministries for nearly thirty years and desires to see hearts made whole.

Dr. A (as she is affectionately known) also holds advanced degrees in divinity, theology, and counseling. This allows her to bring a well-rounded perspective to address spirit, soul, and body. She delights in using a wraparound approach of care with the purpose of aiding people to walk in the abundant life Christ has promised.

Dr. A moves in the offices of teacher, pastor, and prophet and loves the bride of Christ.

CPSIA information can be obtained
at www.ICGtesting.com
Printed in the USA
FSHW011259110421

9 781098 081966

Are you curious about the supernatural realm and the various manifestations of the Holy Spirit? Do you want to learn more about the unique streams of the prophetic ministry? Come and explore the following:

- How to discern the voice of God
- How to test the spirits
- How to accurately represent the King and the kingdom
- How to distinguish a false prophet from a real one
- How woundedness affects a prophetic flow
- How God prepares a prophetic vessel

Prophetic Supernatural Streams is a book designed to restore honor back to prophetic ministry and help young prophetic voices mature in the body of Christ. This book will awaken readers to the spirit realm and acquaint them with the various manifestations of the Holy Spirit.

April Griseta is a doctor of ministry and holds a license to practice mental health counseling. She also copastors New and Lively Hope Ministries with her husband Joe. April is a sought out national conference speaker and hosts the popular TV program *Bounce Back* on Christian Television Network. She has moved in both the prophetic and deliverance ministries for nearly thirty years and desires to see hearts made whole.

Dr. A (as she is affectionately known) also holds advanced degrees in divinity, theology, and counseling. This allows her to bring a well-rounded perspective to address spirit, soul, and body. She delights in using a wraparound approach of care with the purpose of aiding people to walk in the abundant life Christ has promised.

Dr. A moves in the offices of teacher, pastor, and prophet and loves the bride of Christ.

$12.95

ISBN 978-1-0980-8196-6
51295

Christian Faith
PUBLISHING

9 781098 081966

The Addiction of
Mary Todd Lincoln

ANNE E. BEIDLER